To Cathy & I
     from
        Grandmother
          Christmas 1969

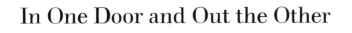

In One Door and Out the Other

In One Door
and Out the Other

A BOOK OF POEMS

by Aileen Fisher

Illustrated by Lillian Hoban

Thomas Y. Crowell Company
New York

More than half the verses in this book are new. Some old favorites were originally published in *The Coffee-Pot Face, Inside a Little House,* and *That's Why,* copyright 1933 (renewed 1960), 1938 (renewed 1965), and 1946 by Aileen Fisher. "Frosted-Window World" and "New Dollhouse" first appeared in *Story Parade,* copyright 1952 and 1950 by Story Parade, Inc. "Christmas Tree" and "Knowing" were first published in *My Weekly Reader,* copyright © 1967 and 1965 by Xerox Corporation, and used by permission of American Education Publications/A Xerox Company, publisher of *My Weekly Reader.* "At Christmas Time" first appeared in *The Instructor,* copyright © 1964 by The Instructor Publications, Inc.

Designed by Bert Clarke Design Group.
Manufactured in the United States of America
L.C. Card 70–81949
1   2   3   4   5   6   7   8   9   10

To Les and Kay
Lucia and Charles
Beth and Dick,
remembering

Contents

In one door
and out the other!
Ring around the tree!
Every minute
something doing . . .
come along and see.

In One Door and Out the Other

FIRST-ING

Out we go
when the buds are bursting
early in spring
for a game of first-ing:

The first green shoots!
The first brown puddle!
The first yellow crocuses
in a huddle!
The first queen bee!
A jonquil growing!
The first forsythia color
showing!

Spring arrives
without much warning,
so we go first-ing
the first bright morning.

DREAMS

Dreams are funny:
they melt all up
like Mother's sugar
in her coffee cup.

BEFORE BREAKFAST

Mother has to comb her hair,
Father has to shave,
but I keep getting hungry
with the time I save.

RUN IN THE RAIN

I wore a newspaper raincoat,
I wore a newspaper hat,
and my feet
went spattering down the street
as fast as the rain could spat.

I must have looked rather funny,
but oh, the race was sport,
and when I dashed
to the door at last
I bet I dripped a *quart*.

ALL-DAY SUCKER

~~~~~~~~~~~~~~~

Somebody was mistaken,
somebody was wrong:
NOBODY's all-day sucker
lasts THAT long.

PLANS

~~~~~~~~~~~~~~~

When I make Plans
that are grand and vast,
even more grand than
the time-before-last,
how can my Mother
say "NO!" so fast?

GOING DOWN THE STREET

When I'm going
on an errand
for my mother
down the street,
I wonder
where *they're* going,
all the people
that I meet.
To the office?
To the market?
To a fancy place
to eat?

I get thinking . . .
does that lady
have a baby?
Or a pet?

Does that carpenter
have color
in his
television set?
And so sometimes
what my mother
sends me after . . .
I forget!

WHISTLING

Cinda came
up close to hear

How my whistle
sounded NEAR.

And she said,
"I never knew

"You had birds
inside of you."

And poor Cinda
almost cried,

Wishing SHE
had birds inside.

PEEKING

〰〰〰〰〰〰〰

When Father is napping
we're quiet as mice.
We sneak in to see him
so peaceful and nice.

But if there's a squeaking
of shoes, or a creaking
of floors, we go streaking
without looking twice.

COMPANY CLOTHES

I had to dress up
and not wear jeans
or even my comfortable
in-betweens,
and not wear boots
or my zebra sweater
because Mother said
she'd had a letter
and someone she knew
when she was small
was stopping to call
so I had to look better.

And what do you know!
Their boy was John . . .
and he had jeans
and a sweater on!
So I changed mine back
in one-two-three,
to keep my company
company.

WAITING

How many times
   can I
   count
   to ten,

How many times
   can I
   jump rope
   when

I'm waiting for Mother
   to
   call
   again?

FRECKLES

Jerry has freckles,
peppered like spice.

And Jerry has a pony
I rode on twice.

I think freckles
are *awfully* nice.

KNOWING

Nobody teaches
a bird to sing
or a frog to croak
as soon as it's spring.

Nobody teaches
a bee to make honey
or shows how-to-hop
to a new little bunny.

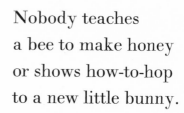

Nobody teaches
a spider to spin . . .
How do they know
what to do to *begin*?

NEW NEIGHBORS

When Smiths packed up
and moved away,
and Judy was gone,
I cried all day.

I knew I'd *never*
like anyone
as much as Judy
or have such fun.

Then Browns moved in
with a silky cat
and a dog with puppies.
Imagine that!

And a girl named Becky . . .
and I forgot
all about missing
Judy a lot.

COME ALONG

wwwwwwwwww

Come along and I'll show you:
here's where a snake went past.
I stopped and let him do it,
and he did it nice and fast.

Here's the hole of a spider.
I saw him going down.
And *here's* where toadstools overnight
grew hats of brassy brown.

Here's where I spilled the bucket
and got my sandals wet.
And *here's* a house for a rabbit . . .
He hasn't
found it
yet.

GROWING

wwwwwwwww

When I ask Mother
she doesn't really know:
"What's inside of me
making me grow?"

So I ask Father
who doesn't grow a bit:
"What's inside of YOU
making you quit?"

And Father says, "Hmmm . . .
I'm—busy—now, Son . . ."
So I STILL don't know
how growing is done.

WHISPERS

Kevin's whispers
buzz in my ear
like a buzzy old bee
too loud to hear.

Darcy's whispers
sound like a breeze
lost in the tops
of faraway trees.

Kathy's never
leave room for doubt,
but *she* hasn't much
to whisper about.

TIGHTROPE WALKER

If I were the spider
walking there
on a thread of silk
in a world of air,

Above all blue,
and beneath all brown,
I'd get so dizzy
I'd fall right down.

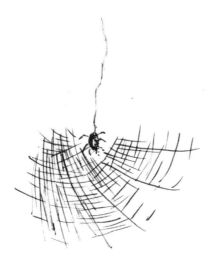

I'LL BE A BAKER

I'll be a baker and run a bakery shop.
I'll bake cookies and never-ever stop.
"No, ma'am . . . out of bread.
Have a layer cake instead!
Have a chocolate cooky spread
with cocoanut on top."

I'll bake pastry all the day long
and put in raisins that maybe don't belong.
"No, ma'am . . . not a bun.
Try a crusty pie for fun!
I've sampled EVERY ONE . . .
you can't go wrong."

I'll be a baker as soon as I am grown.

"A baker?" mumbles Father, in a curious tone.

"You ought to be a doctor
or a lawyer or a chief
or a banker or a broker,
but a BAKER—good grief!
You ought to want an office
with a desk and telephone . . ."

But I'LL be a baker
for reasons of my own.

MEANIE

Susie boasted she could sing
as sweetly as a bird.

"Yes," I said, "I think you can,
from all that I have heard.

"You sing exactly like a crow,
a magpie, or a jay."

And Susie said, "You meanie, you!"
And took her bike away.

PICNICS

Picnics in a box are nice,
with bread and peanut butter,
but *campfire* picnics are the best
when wieners split and sputter.

Cheese and jelly-bread are good,
but toasted buns are better . . .
and for a week
I still can smell
the campfire on my sweater.

FAIRY TALE

I read in a book of a daughter who
made three wishes that all came true.

So I wished my mother would call, "Come, quick,
there's a spoon and a frosting bowl to lick."

And I wished my mother would call, "Make haste!
Here's a nice hot cooky for you to taste."

And I wished my mother would say, "Why, ye-es,
it's foolish to practice your scales, I guess."

I wished, and wished—but I must admit
it didn't work out like the book a BIT.

BIRTHDAY

ᴧᴧᴧᴧᴧᴧᴧᴧᴧᴧᴧᴧ

The next best thing to Christmas,
the next best day to prize
is a birthday, when you're special
in everybody's eyes.

The next best thing to Christmas
if it's summer, spring, or fall,
is a birthday with a party
and a birthday cake and all.

NEW DOLLHOUSE

∿∿∿∿∿∿∿∿∿

Oh, the little roses
on the paper on the wall,
the green and yellow carpet
with its curlicues and all,
the bracket for a jacket
that would hardly fit an elf:
I'd almost like to be a doll
and live inside myself.

Oh, the little cupboard
with the dishes in a row,

the curtains at the windows
that are fastened with a bow,
the table that is able
to be opened twice as wide:
I'd almost like to be a doll
so I could live inside.

Oh, the little sofa
and the padded painted chairs,
the cunning little footstool,
and the candlesticks in pairs,
the places for some vases
on the mantel and the shelf:
I'd almost like to live inside
the little rooms myself.

Oh, the little dresser
and the cozy little bed
with cases on the pillows
and embroidery on the spread,
and the lonely one-and-only
little rocker near the clock:
I'd almost like to be a doll
and sit right down . . . and rock.

IF I WERE MY MOTHER

If I were my mother
I rarely would make
omelet, or parsnips,
or spinach, or steak,
or carrots, or onions—
I'd much rather bake
doughnuts and pudding
and dumplings and cake.

I'd not take the trouble
to cut up a lot
of turnips—instead I'd
make jam in a pot,
and fritters, and cookies,
and pies piping hot . . .
if I were my mother.
Too bad that I'm not!

FOR INSTANCE

Mother gets funny ideas, she does.
    And Father gets them too.
Last night, for instance, the trouble was
they thought I couldn't eat cake because
they thought I must have an ache because
    I couldn't eat oyster stew.

THE FROG AND I

The frog and I,
the frog and I
can sing and hop
but cannot fly.

We both can dive,
we both can swim
(although I can't
compete with him).

We both have skin
that's on to stay,
but mine's not *green*,
I'm glad to say.

SO STILL

When Father says,
"I've had my fill
of so much noise and clatter!"

Then Mother says,
"You sit so still . . .
can something be the matter?"

A DRINK

I always let Peter
work it first
when we find a fountain
and have a thirst,
so then if it squirts
I'll know the worst.

UN-BIRTHDAY PARTY

It wasn't someone's birthday,
but we made a brownish cake
with a clothespin for a candle
and the nuts that pebbles make,
and we put it in the summer sun
to crispy-up and bake.

We wrapped up pine-cone presents
in the nicest way we could,
and maple leaves were place cards,
and favors—twigs of wood . . .
and for not being someone's birthday
it was almost just as good.

DRESSING

It would be easier, of course,
to dress like any cow or horse:

No zipping-up or zipping-down
or changing clothes to go to town,

No snapping-on or hooking-in
or itchy collars at your chin,

No putting-on or taking-off
or bundling-up to stop a cough.

It would be easier, of course,
but then, who'd BE a cow or horse?

NOBODY'S NICER

~~~~~~~~~~~~~~~~

Nobody's nicer
than Mrs. King.

She came to visit
one day in spring,
and let me flash
with her diamond ring.

And even better,
she let me wear
her amber comb
in my yellow hair.

But best of all . . .
you should have seen!
I tried on her earrings,
and looked *sixteen*.

A CANE

If I had a cane
like Grandfather Grimm,
I wouldn't just use it
for walking, like him.

I'd poke it in puddles.
I'd write on the sand.
I'd balance it straight
on the palm of my hand.

I'd aim at a magpie.
I'd swash at the hay.
I'd groove little ditches
and rivers. Why, SAY . . .

If I had a cane
like Grandfather Grimm
I NEVER would use it
for walking, like him.

STAYING OVERNIGHT

∿∿∿∿∿∿∿∿∿

For dinner at Donna's
we had green peas.
At home I'm not very fond of these.
But I ate them all
'cause company should.
And what do you think?
They tasted good.

For breakfast at Donna's
we had oatmeal.
I've never been fond of its taste or feel.
But there wasn't a choice
of oatmeal OR . . .
And what do you think?
I asked for more.

MOTHER'S PARTY

"What's your age?"
  and
"What's your name?"
EVERY lady was the same,
every single one that came:
"What's your age?"
  and
"What's your name?"

No one saw my rubber boots.
Or the way my agate shoots.
No one saw my mouse's cage.
"What's your name?"
  and
"What's your age?"

No one saw my studded belt.
No one saw the way-I-felt.

No one saw my glider game.
EVERY lady was the same,
every single one that came:
"What's your age?"
  and
"What's your name?"

THE RACE

My tricycle's a camel
With thickly padded feet.

My wagon is a charger
That clatters down the street.

I'd like to ride them both at once
To see which one would beat.

FRANCIE AND I

Francie said when she was three
and came one day to play with me:
"Fur grows on a bumblebee."

Francie said when she was four
and came to play with me some more:
"Flowers come up without a door."

Francie said when she was five:
"Rivers surely are alive . . .
they can run and swim and dive."

I am not a bit like Francie.
I can't think of things so fancy.
But I know some secret places,
and I'm good at *making faces*.

COMPANY

Mother has company
and frosted cakes.

And very little sandwiches
that Lottie makes.

Mother has nut cups
tied with a bow.

I WISH the company
would have to go.

TALKING

When company is talking
(and talking's what they do)
my father tells a lot of things
I never knew he knew.

MEASLES

ᴧᴧᴧᴧᴧᴧᴧᴧᴧᴧᴧᴧᴧ

When I had measles
I dreamed a lot
of things that I
would rather have not.

And though I tried,
I never could seem
to dream of what
I rather would dream.

MY DOG GINGER

He's reddish
and brownish,
like gingersnap spice.

He's eager
and clownish
and silky and nice.

And when it comes
to kissing me
when he is full
of missing me,
he never stops
at only once
or even only twice.

PEEKING IN

When company came
we peeked in the door
(Rebecca and I)
and squeaked on the floor,
then giggled and ran,
and peeked in once more.

I opened the door
by lifting the hook,
and Becky fell in . . .
the tumble she took!
And *she* got a cooky,
and *I* got a Look.

FALL SURPRISES

mmmmmmmm

I never know
till the leaves shake free
if a bird nest hides
in the poplar tree.

I never know
till the vines are bare
if wasps built a papery house
in there.

I never guess
till the leaves have blown
how much there is
I never have known.

JELLY BEANS

"I like white ones."

"Here are two."

"I like blacks."

"But there are so few!"

"I want pink ones."

"Two for you."

"I like orange."

"WHAT shall we do—
there isn't an orange,
I've looked them through."

"Awwww."

"Wait! here's a red,
and a yellow too—
THAT'LL make orange
when you get through."

VISITORS

When people
come to see us
and sit around on chairs,
do they wonder
what our house is like
in all the rooms upstairs?

Do they wonder
what's in closets
that everybody wears,
and what's on all
our cupboard shelves?

I wonder about *theirs*.

DOWN

Down on the rooftops,
down on the eaves,
down on the patio
fall the leaves.

Down on the stoop
and the window sill
bright leaves flutter
and dry leaves spill.

And down I sink
in a soft deep bed
of brown and yellow
and crackly red.

SEPTEMBER

ⵯⵯⵯⵯⵯⵯⵯⵯ

"Brownie, it isn't my fault.
Summer just came to a halt.
Now that the weather is cool,
Brownie,
     I'm going to school.

"Brownie, you lie in the sun
after some sniffs and a run.
No, you can't come. It's a rule.
Brownie,
     I'm going to school."

COASTER WAGON

Down the hill in our wagon we go,
bumpity, bump, bump, bump—
over the stones with squeaks and groans
and jolts that reach to the ends of our bones,
down the hill in our wagon we go—
      bump
bumpity   bump
          BUMP.

Our wagon is not a streamlined one,
bumpity, bump, bump, bump—
it's stiff in the joints, but it still can run,
and we go pretty fast when we've once begun;
our wagon is old, but it's lots of fun—
      bump
bumpity   BUMP.
       bump

CONSOLATION

When Mother says, "No.
Your brother is older . . .
your head doesn't go
as high as his shoulder.
You can't tag along,
and you know I'm right,"
I don't feel as sad
as I otherwise might . . .

For I have a cat
with kittens (three),
and a guinea pig
who depends on me,
and a wag-tail dog
as high as my knee
I *like* to have tagging
along with me.

GOLDFISH

I have
four fish
with poppy eyes—

Awfully
poppy
for their size—

Perhaps
they're poppy
from surprise:

For after
frisking
in a sea,

Fish must
think it
queer to be

Looking
through a
glass—at Me.

THANKSGIVING DINNER

ⱽⱽⱽⱽⱽⱽⱽⱽⱽⱽⱽⱽⱽⱽⱽⱽⱽ

With company coming,
there's always *before*:
shine up the silver,
sweep up the floor,
corn and red peppers
to hang by the door,
salad to garnish
and water to pour,
sample the dressing
and gravy once more . . .
Listen!
They're coming!
Oh, run to the door!

WHITE MORNING

〰〰〰〰〰〰

Everything was white as white,
every roof and yard in sight.

Snow filled all the garden chairs
with white and humpy teddy bears.

Evergreens wore woolly wraps
with white and fluffy mitts and caps,

And up and down and left and right
all the world was white as white,

Excepting me . . . for Mother said
when I came in for honey-bread:
"Goodness, but your cheeks are *red*."

MUSIC BOX

wwwwwwwwww

The music box
will make a sound
as long as it is wound and wound.

But I make noises,
big and small,
without a winding up at all.

The music box
runs down itself
when it's forgotten on the shelf,

But Mother's all
that hinders me
from making noise continually.

SNOW PICTURES

∿∿∿∿∿∿∿∿∿

Rick draws rabbits on the snow,
and sometimes he draws cats.
Nancy Ann draws other things,
like butterflies and bats.

I can't draw an animal
of any shape or size.
But I can draw *potatoes*, though,
and poke them full of eyes.

WINTER DAY

ꟷꟷꟷꟷꟷ

You make a snowman
and put a necktie on it.

I'll make a snow*ma'am*
and have her wear a bonnet.

WINTER WALK

I like days in winter
when paths are packed with snow
and feet make creaky footsteps
wherever footsteps go,
      and
I like days in winter
when snow lies soft and deep
and footsteps go so quietly
you'd think they were asleep.

A WONDERFUL MAN

My father carries a pearl-handled knife
with three steel blades that are big as life:
one is longest, and one is littler,
but the shortest one is the sharpest whittler.

My father whittles me whistles from sticks,
and uses his knife when there're things to fix,
and he whittles me darts and arrows with wings
and sailboats and rabbits and other such things.

And sometimes he asks me, "Would *you* like to try
to whittle a little with me standing by?"
So I whittle something as well as I can . . .
Say, but my father's a wonderful man!

FROSTED-WINDOW WORLD

The strangest thing,
the strangest thing
came true for me today:
I left myself beneath the quilt
and softly slipped away.

And do you know
the place I went
as shyly as a mouse,
as curious as a cottontail,
as watchful as a grouse?
Inside the frosted windowpane
(it's rather puzzling to explain)
to visit Winter's house!

How bright it was.
How light it was.
How white it was all over,
with twists and turns
through frosted ferns
and crusted weeds and clover,
through frost-grass
reaching to my knees,

and frost-flowers
thick on all the trees.

The brightest sights,
the whitest sights
kept opening all around,
for everything
was flaked with frost,
the plants, the rocks,
the ground,
and everything was breathless-still
beneath the crusty rime—
there wasn't any clock to tick
or any bell to chime.
Inside the frosted windowpane
(it's rather puzzling to explain)
there wasn't any Time.

How clear it was.
How queer it was.
How near it was to heaven!
Till someone came
and called my name
and said, "It's after seven!"
And heaven vanished like an elf
and I whisked back, inside myself.

WINTER

~~~~~~~~~~~~~~

Winter doesn't have picnics
under the bright green leaves,

But winter has daggers of icicles
that dangle from the eaves.

Winter doesn't have swimming,
or camping, or balls to bat,

But winter has Christmas, and nothing,
nothing is better than that.

AT CHRISTMAS TIME

In every house on every street
around and up and down
there's something special going on,
in every house in town:

Gifts to make
and lights to string
and sweets to bake
and bells to ring
(with snowflakes sifting down),
and shiny eyes
and dancy feet
in every house on every street,
on every street in town.

CHRISTMAS TREE

My kitten thinks
the Christmas tree
is more than something
just to see.

She taps the balls
of green and red,
and swings the tinsel
overhead,

And rings the bells,
and starts to purr
as if we'd trimmed it
all for her.

BEDTIME

Father
stays up very late—
we often
hear his voice.

WE always
go to bed at eight . . .
but not
from choice!

GOOD NIGHT

wwwwwwwww

This day's done.
Tomorrow's another.

Good night, Daddy.
Good night, Mother.

Good night, kitten,
book, and brother . . .

In one dream
and out the other.

About the Author

Aileen Fisher lives in a cabin on a ranch in the foothills of Colorado —a cabin that she helped build with her own hands. From the window at her desk she looks beyond fields and pine-covered hills to Arapahoe Peak.

Miss Fisher was born on the Upper Peninsula of Michigan. When she was five, her family moved to a farm near Iron River, and it was there that she learned to love the outdoors and to look forward to the changing seasons. Her first poetry was written for the high school column of the local newspaper. Since that time she has written many books and plays for children. She attended the University of Chicago and later received a degree in journalism from the University of Missouri.

About the Illustrator

Lillian Hoban has illustrated a great many books for boys and girls, and her drawings are in permanent collections at the Free Library of Philadelphia, the University of Minnesota, and the University of Mississippi. Mrs. Hoban was born in Philadelphia and studied at the Graphic Sketch Club and the Philadelphia Museum School.

Mrs. Hoban and her husband and four children live in Wilton, Connecticut.